the ties that bind

A Biblical Handbook on Soul Ties

Published by Active-Faith.org

Copyright 2024 by Charli Caraway. All rights reserved worldwide. No part of this book may be reproduced or transmitted in any form or by any means electronic or mechanical, including photocopying, recording or by any information storage and retrieval system without written permission from Charli Caraway.

Printed in the United States of America

ISBN: 9-798-88311-794-6

Books › Religion & Spirituality › Christian Books & Bibles › Christian Living › Personal Growth

Charli Caraway *The Ties That Bind* Disclaimer/Warning: This book is intended for lecture and informative purposes only. This publication is designed to provide competent and reliable information regarding the subject matter covered. The author or publisher are not engaged in rendering legal or professional advice. Laws vary from state to state and if legal, financial, or other expert assistance is needed, the services of a professional should be sought. The author and publisher disclaim any liability that is incurred from the use or application of the contents of this book.

Table of Contents

Introduction - 5

Chapter 1 - 9

Chapter 2 - 21

Chapter 3 - 39

Chapter 4 - 53

Warning - 57

Introduction

Going to the salon or the barber shop is always an interesting experience. First, you are always privy to seeing people at their less-than-best. After all, everyone there is expecting to leave looking better, right? There are also the tidbits of conversations you hear from other chairs. The random, and often sad, renditions of life's greatest and worst events.

A few years ago, I was sitting in the chair of my favorite stylist. It was an early Monday morning appointment, and strangely, the salon was empty. It was just me and my stylist. It didn't take but a few minutes in her chair for me to realize that something was off. At first, I thought she was angry with me. Then, I thought she might just be angry at my hair. But then I realized, it was a much deeper issue, and she was struggling.

In order to save my scalp, I said, "STOP!" She paused, hands in mid-air. I spun the chair around. "Something isn't right with you today. Your soul is troubled! How can I pray for you?" And the tears came. Lots and lots of tears. I quickly realized there were several issues that had been piling up.

She explained that she loves, literally LOVES, her clients. She uses her chair to encourage and speak the Word of God over her clients as much as she can. However, they share so much with her that each day she is leaving with the weight of their situations bearing down on her. Then, at home she has all the other issues of home life to deal with as well. The combination of it all was becoming too much and she felt like she was choking.

I think there are so many of us that do the same thing. We get lost in the details because of the weight of the details. However, there is a simple and effective way to pray that makes it all much more manageable. That day, I taught her about soul ties.

After a brief explanation of soul ties and how they were manifesting in her life she agreed, that was definitely her problem. Of course, the solution was a simple prayer and the world was right again!

Now, each day (and I check in with her every 6-8 weeks) she confirms that she is still breaking unnecessary soul ties and living in the freedom of this.

This book is designed to help you as well. Sometimes, it is the simplest thing that is most profound. This simple handbook is designed to teach, explain, and provide solutions for everyday challenges we all face that are connected to our souls.

Chapter 1
What is a Soul Tie?

When I think about ties that bind, I think of many things. Corsets, Japanese foot binding, bondage, prisoners tied up. However, I also think of shoelaces, boat knots, parachute lines, and the way my granny used to make macrame.

I remember the first time I ever heard a Bible teacher say, "If you slept with someone prior to getting married, it is likely that he/she is still linked to you when you have sex with your husband/wife." To say I was shocked was an understatement. I didn't understand. HOW were they PRESENT?

This Bible teacher was trying to explain that soul ties are invisible attachments linked to memories and emotions that will very likely show up when you are engaged in emotional behavior with someone else. That may sound confusing, but I will explain.

First, it is important to explain the difference between the spirit and the soul. We are born with both. However, it is our soul that tends to get us in trouble. It is the place from which we sin. The Spirit is different. When we accept Christ as our savior, our spirit is renewed and perfect through Christ Jesus.

Ironically, you will not find the phrase "soul ties" in the Bible. You will only find evidence of them. It is modern terminology taken from Biblical verbiage. The first and most direct reference is recorded by the prophet Samuel. Jonathan's soul was "knit to the soul of David." That phrase is the closest wording we have to "soul ties" and is actually in 1 Samuel 18:1-4:

"Now when he had finished speaking to Saul, the soul of Jonathan was knit to the soul of David, and Jonathan loved him as his own soul… Then Jonathan and David made a covenant, because he loved him as his own soul."

Technically, "soul ties" is modern terminology for a spiritual situation. Don't get lost in the verbiage. Through a decade of teaching about this issue, many think that soul ties are merely formed in sexual relationships. And, yes, they are most certainly formed in any intimate relationship – Samson's soul tie with Delilah was his downfall – more on that later. But the terminology should be examined more closely.

A "soul tie" is found in the soul and it is an invisible link to another person or many people that you carry with you wherever you go, into whatever situation you find yourself in. A soul "tie" connects you to someone emotionally and spiritually.

There are healthy and unhealthy soul ties. Some teachers refer to them as godly and ungodly soul ties. Either way, they are there. The vocabulary choice doesn't change the existence.

WHAT IS THE SOUL?

What is the soul? The soul is comprised of the mind, the will, and emotion. It is mentioned in the Bible (KJV) more than 500 times. The soul is mentioned in 27 Old Testament books, and 15 New Testament books. God must have thought it pretty significant!

Throughout the Bible, the word "soul" has only four translations. Yet, each translation means "life; life force; immaterial part of a person; psyche; seat of emotion and desire the mind or inner person, or state of dignity." (Strongs, 2001) They each relate in some way to our mental health.

The mind is how we think. The will is how we make decisions, an exercise of our will. And emotions are self-explanatory. We ALL have emotions, and they often drive our thoughts and decision-making.

Therefore, any relationship in which you exercise logic, free choice, and/or emotion develops soul ties. I often joke that you can have soul ties with whom you've shared oxygen. Some soul ties are stronger than others – like in sexual relationships. However, there are very strong ties with family members, business colleagues, and any other person that invokes strong emotion in you. We also experience soul ties in the church.

Remember my stylist mentioned in the introduction? Her clients had invoked compassion which is rooted in emotional connection. This is no different than a counselor, a teacher, a medical professional, or someone in ministry. It is also seen in every family relationship we have. And yes, it can be seen in every professional – even an accounting office. How? What about the end of the month when reports are due? Aren't there emotional stressors involved? What about tax time? Anyone that shares in the emotions of an event can share a soul tie.

HOW DO WE KNOW IF WE HAVE SOUL TIES?

How does one recognize a soul tie? Consider these questions:

- Do you desire to change the nature or boundaries of a relationship but there is some inexplicable guilt or fear that keeps you from doing so?
- Are you stressed and/or losing sleep because you are plagued by words said or situations you've experienced with someone?
- Do you have feelings of heaviness and responsibility over someone else's choices or actions?
- Do you think of a significant other from your past when you are intimate with your partner?
- Are you experiencing indescribable emotions towards someone (love, anger, resentment, guilt, etc.)?

- Have you experienced roller-coaster emotions with someone – highs and lows (including trauma)?
- Do you make unwise decisions about relationships despite the fact that you know it's unwise?
- Do you have an unexplained desire to stay in a relationship or business partnership but it isn't logical?

If you can answer "yes" to any of these questions you have a soul tie. This is not an exhaustive list. It is merely a list designed to provoke thought about your relationships from a different perspective.

If left unaddressed, soul ties can begin to affect our lives in very serious ways. They will affect our ability to mentally process, our rest, our peace, and our effectiveness as Christians in a dark world that needs our light! If ignored, soul ties can actually bind us and minimize our joy potential.

Remember, 3 John 2 says, *"Beloved I pray that you may prosper and be in health, even as your soul prospers."* The soul cannot prosper when it is linked to something that weighs it down. Prosperity soars. Any unhealthy soul tie will just keep you tethered and unable to ride the winds of freedom.

An example of good soul ties is Jonathan and David from 1 Samuel 18. An example of bad soul ties would be Samson and Delilah from Judges 16.

I've heard people say they believed all soul ties were bad. I would disagree. I've heard others say that they didn't want to break soul ties because they thought doing so would sever the relationship completely (like in a marriage or family or business partnership). At one time, I also was confused about severing relationships if I severed a soul tie. There is a way to address this as well which will be addressed in a later chapter.

Soul ties can be a controversial topic in the body of Christ. Let me just say this. I've lived this, as you will see. I am very transparent. And I never teach anything that I can't back up with scripture. It was a weird and wonderful path that led me to this teaching, and I hope that it will bless you.

NEGATIVE AFFECTS OF SOUL TIES

Soul ties can lead to a lapse in good judgement.

Judges 16:16 "And it came to pass when she pestered him daily with her words and pressed him, so that his soul was vexed to death."

This quote comes from the middle of the story about Samson and Delilah. There is significant detail about this story that I discuss in *The Wounded Warrior* which is about soul wounds, covering much deeper, more serious issues with the soul that have become strongholds. However, this one snippet of text can reach beyond this one story and relate to so many.

This story is also about a sexual relationship that should not have evolved the way it did. It, too, was of a sinful nature. However, my point in highlighting it is that when we have soul ties with someone – anyone – that gives the other person a spiritual influence over us which can affect our decision-making and logic greatly.

Even the world outside of the Bible and Christianity has romanticized the story of Samson and Delilah. It was a forbidden relationship. He had super-human strength which God used to fight His enemies. Delilah was persuaded by God's enemies to pester Samson with constant questioning about where his strength (and thus his threat) came from.

Samson knew it was the fact that he had never cut his hair. He had been dedicated as a Nazarite as a child which meant he couldn't cut his hair. Delilah was already in an intimate relationship with him when she began her ploys. He was able to put her off with false responses for a while. However, you will notice in verse 16 that his soul was finally "vexed to death". He finally told her the truth and she cut his hair in his sleep. It led to his imprisonment and death.

Why is this story so important? Because bad soul ties weaken our judgement and minimize wisdom in our decisions. It can be in a relationship at work, within a friend group, within family, or even within the church.

More than once I have been plagued with the weight of knowing what the "right" course of action was, but I couldn't carry it out because of an unhealthy soul tie I had with someone that right course of action would negatively affect.

Once, I had a woman working for me that I greatly loved. Her job performance began to go down and I knew she needed to be fired. However, I knew her whole family, even her children. We had soul ties and I was severely struggling with the concept of firing her because of this. I loved her, but her job performance was not acceptable. I prayed for wisdom one day and the Lord reminded me to break unhealthy soul ties with her.

I did, and that day I was kindly, but firmly able to fire her without feeling the weight of the issue. I am grateful that we are still friends today!

Chapter 2
Soul Ties In The Bible

God was serious about the soul. He created it from the very beginning. Genesis 2:7 says, "And the LORD God formed man of the dust of the ground and breathed into his nostrils the breath of life; and man became a living soul." (KJV)

This soul gave man free will. When Adam and Eve took of the fruit of the tree of the knowledge of good and evil, they made a choice (Genesis, chapter 3). They exercised logic and free will. In doing so, they opened up a world of sin. It is first evidenced when Adam says he was "afraid" in Genesis 3:10. There it is, man's first use of free will and his first experience with emotion.

Of course, the thoughts, will and emotions of man have continued to drive us all down paths of sinfulness. Truly, the soul is the epicenter of sin. The Bible is filled with one bad decision after another. And our emotions very often drive those decisions.

These truths can make our life weary. After repetitive mistakes, bad choices, and misplaced emotions we have feel heavy and helpless. However, God wants to lift the heaviness our soul feels. This is what God said through Jeremiah about the souls of his people:

Jeremiah 31:25, *"For I have satiated the weary soul, and I have replenished every sorrowful soul."* This is His heart for his children.

We see soul ties in many different kinds of relationships.

FRIENDSHIP

The best example of a soul tie through friendship is Jonathan and David: 1 Sam. 18:1

"Now when he had finished speaking to Saul, the [a]soul of Jonathan was knit to the soul of David, and Jonathan loved him as his own soul."

This soul tie would act as a bonding agent between the men that would affect the kingdom and their families for generations to come. This particular soul tie brought David comfort in a time when Saul hunted him like an outlaw. When David felt betrayed by someone he'd served faithfully, he could lean on this tie with Jonathan. Jonathan saved his life.

Later, when Saul and Jonathan both die in battle (1 Samuel 31), David grieves both of them greatly (2 Samuel 1). However, the greater effect of this healthy soul tie comes into perspective in 2 Samuel 9. David learns that there is a son of Jonathan's that still lives. And, despite the fact that he is disabled, provides him Jonathan's fortune and place at the king's table his whole life.

This is such a good example of a healthy, beneficial soul tie through friendship.

FAMILY

A soul tie through family can be seen between Joseph and his brothers. In Gensis 37, Joseph's brothers throw him in a pit and sell him into slavery. We know very little of what happened between the brothers until a famine forces them to go to Egypt in Genesis 42. We see their "soul tie" become evident in Genesis 42:21. They stand discussing their situation in the famine before Joseph. Not realizing that Joseph has lived, sits before them, and can understand their private conversation in their first tongue, they discuss their situation. In verse 21 they say, "We are truly guilty concerning our brother, for we saw the anguish of his soul when he pleaded with us and we would not hear; therefore this distress has come upon us."

The soul link is clearly stated. Joseph was experiencing heartbreaking family disappointment. Family, due to the close nature and relationships, often have soul ties. Whether they are ties created in moments of joy and celebration, or moments of distress and hurt – family creates soul ties.

In the middle of the same story, Genesis 44:30, the brothers are standing before Joseph and they clearly say that Benjamin's life is "tied" to Jacob's. Indicating a deep and spiritual relationship.

It is important to note here that family soul ties can be healthy AND unhealthy. We can experience both at the same time and this will be discussed in a later chapter because, needless to say, we don't want the unhealthy soul ties to dampen or squash the healthy soul ties.

Sometimes we share blood with toxic people. Sometimes our circumstances dictate that we live with them. The Psalms discuss this.

Psalm 120:6, "My Soul has dwelt too long with one who hates peace."

Ouch. God always has a way of helping us realizes that he sees us. He knows what we are dealing with.

Think for a minute about all the emotions we experience in a family context. Think about all the decision-making that we teach or exercise in the family context. It can be parent to child, spouse to spouse, parent to grandparent, and extended family is also involved in many situations. Aunts, uncles, cousins, etc.

In families we experience highs and lows, celebrations and disappointments. We have birth and death. We gain family members through marriage, and we lose family members through distance. We plan celebrations but worry about what the one person will say the whole time. We get caught up in trying to set healthy boundaries with certain people coming into our homes. Sometimes a spouse can be less tolerant of your family than you are – and it's probably because they don't have the soul ties that you do!

Navigating family – children to third cousins – is much easier when we can prayerfully navigate soul ties in the relationship.

Due to a divorce situation and ongoing negative relations with my "starter husband", my relationship with my three biological children was extremely strained. Hurtful words and actions lingered with me. My children responded to me in conversations with severe toxicity. Now, there were many things to be reconciled and redeemed there. However, it started when I began recognizing that there were negative soul ties and healthy soul ties. When I started breaking the negative soul ties, little by little, things started turning around.

Imagine a large ship trying to turn and head out to sea in a large port. However, the ship can't turn because it's still tied to the loading dock. No matter how much power the engines exert, the tethered ship can't maneuver because it's tied down. No matter how much power the captain applies to turning from the dock, the ship's infrastructure will be challenged and strained. The dock, also, will experience strain and possibly structural damage. This is what happens in relationships when we operate under soul ties that are unhealthy.

SEX & INTIMACY

Soul ties can be created through sex and intimacy.

Marriage between believers is the epitome of a healthy soul tie. The word "joined" is used in relation to marriage. In Ephesians 5:31 we are told that a man is to be "joined" to his wife. That word "joined" in Greek meant to cleave, stick to, glue or cement.

Then in Matthew 19:6 we read, *"Whatever God has joined together, let no man separate."* Again, we see the word "joined". In this situation it means to be yoked to.

This joining between husband and wife in marriage allows for a spiritual flow.

Consider Genesis 34:1-3, and also verse 8.

"Now Dinah the daughter of Leah, whom she had borne to Jacob, went out to see the daughters of the land. And when Shechem the son of Hamor the Hivite, prince of the country, saw her, he took her and lay with her, and violated her. His soul was

strongly attracted to Dinah the daughter of Jacob, and he loved the young woman and spoke kindly to the young woman.

"But Hamor spoke with them [Jacob, Dinah's father], saying, "The soul of my son Shechem longs for your daughter. Please give her to him as a wife."

First, we cannot escape the fact that the prince raped Dinah. However, the scripture clearly says his soul was attracted to her and that after they had intercourse his soul longed for her. So, the source of his sin was longing for her.

Sadly, we don't get a picture of Dinah's feelings on the matter. This is largely due to the minimized role of women during that time. However, I assure you, Dinah's soul was affected as well. It was inevitable. There is no doubt it was a deeply emotional experience for her.

Later in this story, two of her brothers decided to murder every man in the city of Shechem because they had dishonored Dinah. I imagine that again; her soul was emotional and troubled.

It is easy to see how sex can create a soul tie. I've heard many Christians use 1 Corinthians 6:16 as a scripture explaining soul ties through sex. I disagree with using this scripture as a soul tie explanation. At no point does it mention the soul. In fact, oppositely, is says that two bodies become one flesh. It says nothing about their souls merging. However, it's a little difficult to have sex without emotion. So, we can deduct that they were "tied together" emotionally, but we cannot assume.

I want to stress that even intimacy can create a soul tie. I was teaching about soul ties to a group of men and women in 2023. I wasn't sure how the lesson went because there seemed to be more silence in the room than participation. Before the next class a couple, Don and Deana, came to me and thanked me for teaching about soul ties.

Don shared that he'd lived with a pornography addiction for many years. In fact, they'd once gotten divorced over the issue. However, he'd received healing and therapy and they had remarried. After the lesson on soul ties, he decided to do a little soul tie maintenance (discussed in a later chapter). When he started praying, God convicted him that he had a soul tie with every single woman/person he'd ever watched through porn media. He said after quite some time in prayer he finally felt freedom because he'd broken so many soul ties he was never meant to carry.

I'd never considered before this moment that soul ties could be created through pornography, but they can. Sex is portrayed every where we turn in our society. Even commercials talk openly about sex and portray sexualized ads. In Matthew 5:28 we are told that just looking on a woman with lust is adultery in the heart. This isn't just for men. Women can do the same thing. The emotions invoked when this happens make it a soul tie and it needs to be broken!

MINISTRY

We can see another great example of a healthy soul tie from Paul in Colossians. He is speaking to the church at Colosse and very passionately encouraging them to knit their souls together in love so that they will be able to stand together, strong and courageous, as they live out their faith.

"I want you to know how much I have agonized for you and for the church at Laodicea, and for many other believers who have never met me personally. I want them to be encouraged and knit together by strong ties of love. I want them to have complete confidence that they understand God's mysterious plan, which is Christ himself. ³ In him lie hidden all the treasures of wisdom and knowledge." (NLT)

Paul knew the church would need to be a strong fabric, souls knit together, so that they could support each other and stand strong when trials and cultural kickback came. He wanted them to keep Christ as the center but knew the trials of pioneering the faith. Therefore, he blatantly encouraged this church in Colosse.

Does that mean that the human factor didn't touch them? Of course not. I'm certain that within that body of believers there were some unhealthy soul ties. But it would be an injustice for us not to consider the strength and beauty of healthy soul ties as presented here by Paul.

For 10 years my husband and I had a long-term transitional home for homeless women and children called Restoring Joy Ministries. Working with families in crisis is very challenging. Those women and children came in with all kinds of soul ties and soul wounds (yes, there's a difference!).

However, once they were settled into a place of safety and able to start rebuilding their dignity, they began to develop soul ties that were rooted in our love for Christ Jesus. We ministered to them through the Word of God and helped them get back up on their feet through the provision of God. As these things happened, they developed healthy soul ties with us and the other families in the ministry.

Our ministry shirt was black with simple white letters on the front that said, "Got Joy?" The day I designed those shirts I was in a rush. I needed shirts quickly for an event and thought – I'll just throw something together now and do something better for future events. That never happened.

Those shirts became a brand. Those ladies wore those t-shirts like they were expensive designer fashion. It was because of what they represented – freedom and truth in Jesus. Those t-shirts became a physical manifestation of an unseen soul tie.

In fact, one lady was accused of shoplifting once at Walmart. When I arrived at Walmart to talk to the police and pick her up, she was wearing the black and white t-shirt. The officer told me she had been falsely accused and she was in fact innocent. However, she'd stated to him that she "would NEVER do anything illegal in that t-shirt because it would reflect negatively on everyone associated with Restoring Joy." That, my friends, is a HEALTHY soul tie!

Chapter 3
Eliminating Soul Ties

When I introduce this topic to people, they often assume that it involves a lengthy process or counseling. However, I am here to assure you the process and prayer necessary to manage soul ties is simple, quick, and EFFECTIVE!

God never wanted us to suffer in our soul, although he knew we would because of our nature.

So, God made sure that we knew He would revive, restore, and replenish our souls. David revealed that we must lean on God to restore our soul.

Psalm 23:3 says "He restores my soul". It is not something we can do in our own will the soul contains our will. We must use God's grace!

God knew that our soul could take us to dark places, even death. But he wants us to know he will save us!

Psalm 30:3 "O LORD, You brought my soul up from the grave; You have kept me alive, [a]that I should not go down to the pit."

God never wanted things to be complicated for us. He wanted even soul ties to be addressed simply. His law is perfectly simple. Which makes wisdom attainable. When we have a soul linked only to healthy things and people, the simplicity of our relationship with Him gives us wisdom.

Psalm 19:7 "The instructions of the LORD are perfect, reviving the soul; The decrees of the LORD are trustworthy, making wise the simple" (NLT)

SOUL TIE PRAYER

Before I explain the simple prayer, I want to give you an application context in which I learned to do this. Remember, I said that I had some very strained and painful relationship issues with my three biological children? Please understand, I did not hold them at fault. They were actually the victims in a very toxic situation. However, I needed to pop a hole in that bubble of toxicity.

I learned about soul ties from a great Bible teacher that was explaining the spiritual ramifications of sex. So, it was never on my radar that I had unhealthy soul ties with others in my life. However, one day I was driving on the highway. Highway time has always been a great time for God to speak to me. I was complaining to Him about my family "issues". Suddenly, He said, "break your soul ties with them".

I was floored. First, I doubted it was God's voice because I didn't think it was biblical. Then He began to lead me down the path of what I call "Heaven's Logistics". I was reminded that the soul is the mind, the will, and the emotion. I was reminded that my complaints to Him were all based in decisions, logical (or illogical) circumstances, and the emotions resulting that were tearing me apart.

So, I countered God's voice with my own (faulty) logic: "I don't want to break soul ties with my CHILDREN! I LOVE THEM! I will NEVER have a relationship with them if I break ALL soul ties with them." I'm sure God was rolling His eyes, but he gently said, "Then break the unhealthy soul ties."

I'm sure it took me a good 20 miles to consider that statement. First, I had never heard that there might be soul ties with someone outside of sex. I had also never heard that there might be soul ties in healthy and unhealthy contexts. Can I be honest? I was desperate. I was drained. I was on the verge of delusional with a broken heart for the relationship with my children. So, I did it.

From the depths of my soul I said, "Lord, I break every unhealthy soul tie I have with my children in the name of Jesus!" Then for good measure, I prayed, "But, Lord, I ask that you bless every healthy soul tie I have with them so that you will receive the glory and the honor for our relationship."

That was it. It was over. I felt like I had the weight of the world lifted off of me inside and out.

Later, I got out my Bible, and I began to look for all the scriptures that could possibly teach me about the soul and soul ties. I knew in my heart that I'd done the right thing. But I wanted biblical proof that I'd done the right thing according to the word.

Soon, as life does, I experienced some kickback. More emotion-rendering words and choices that I had to process through. However, I noticed it didn't affect me as much as it had before. I started praying my little soul tie prayer more often. In fact, it became an almost weekly event. In fact, it was usually when I was driving.

Then I noticed when there was conflict with my husband (which, in our house, is referred to as "intense fellowship") I would walk away and pray my soul tie prayer over him. Things would just organically start to work out. Conflict would dissipate. WOW! This was because I chose not to respond with unhealthy emotions or twisted, selfish logic.

I would like to share that my relationships with my children and others did not resolve immediately. However, they immediately began to move in the direction of healing. I have a beautiful relationship with all of my children now. Do they test me? Yes. But now I know what to do!

BREAK THE SOUL TIES

The prayer is simple! And, according to Colossians 3:17, do everything in the name of Jesus. I also encourage everyone to pray OUT LOUD. Satan cannot read our thoughts. I prefer the devil and any of his demons that want to take advantage of my unhealthy soul ties to KNOW they no longer have a spiritually unhealthy place which they can attack.

Pray like this:

Lord, I BREAK every UNHEALTHY soul tie I have with _____ in the name of Jesus.

I also ask that you BLESS every HEALTHY soul tie I have with _____ in the name of Jesus so that in every way you will receive the glory and the honor for the strength and health in our relationship. Amen

***Please note that there are some soul ties that should not and will not be blessed by God. Those soul ties need to be broken

COMPLETELY, FOREVER. God can only bless relationships that are within his law.

Soul ties, unaddressed, can take us down a path of pain that become strongholds called Soul Wounds. It is possible that breaking soul ties will help you, but you may recognize there is a deeper issue. Soul wounds are caused by sin and trauma. Breaking soul ties may not be enough if this is your personal situation. If you'd like to learn more about soul wounds and soul wound healing, please read my book *The Wounded Warrior*.

SOUL TIES WITH DEAD PEOPLE

Just the subtitle is awkward, isn't it? However, I have been through some significant grief. I've lost all my grandparents and my parents. I've lost students (from my teaching days) and I've lost friends young and old. Grief is real.

God, again dealt with me on this issue in prayer before he took me to the Word. And, again, I was driving on the highway. My father had passed weeks before. We had just finished up his memorial service and I was on my way to visit my mother who, at that time, had been living with Alzheimer's for 13 years. She depended on me.

I missed my dad, but I knew he was with the Lord. I knew his faith had been rock-solid and he'd served the Lord well in his life. But there was a weight on me. There was a strong silence that would not shake, and tears would come randomly. I knew the stages of grief and I felt the freedom to cry and miss him. But something in the back of my mind said, "this is spiritual."

I asked the Lord if I needed to repent for anything between my father and myself. Silence. I asked the Lord what the heaviness was that consumed me and kept me from functioning in fullness. I heard it again: "Break soul ties."

By this time, I was already teaching others about healthy and unhealthy soul ties, but this was on a new level. Break soul ties with the dead? Weird? Was that witchcraft? I knew counselors and therapists often ask clients to work through certain exercises where they write letters or make peace with people that have passed on. My father's passing had been difficult. He experienced pain and it was emotional and painful to watch. So, I had been experiencing very strong feelings (emotion) and my decision-making had been in hyperdrive (mind, will). So, I took a deep breath and prayed this prayer:

"Lord, I break every unhealthy soul tie I had with Dad in the name of Jesus. I ask that you bless every healthy soul tie I had with him in the name of Jesus. And Lord, if there is ANYTHING in this prayer that is ungodly and not of You, please forgive me and let my words fall to the ground and not bear fruit. Amen."

It happened again! I felt lighter, free! My whole countenance shifted. When I walked in to see my mother, the nurses asked if I'd had a face lift! I haven't cried for him since that day. I've rejoiced in the many memories made with him. I've rejoiced in things he would find fun and amusing. But I have not shed one tear in grief.

Again, I went to the Word of God. I needed confidence from scripture in what I was praying!

I know people who literally started wasting away physically when they lost a loved one. Their grief became the focus of their thoughts, their decision-making, and their emotions. Nothing else could gain focus because their soul was so consumed with their grief.

Psalm 31:9-10 is a scripture that links the soul and the body to grief and mental/physical duress. It is proof that breaking unhealthy soul ties with the dead is a good idea. *"Have mercy on me, O LORD, for I am in trouble;*

My eye wastes away with grief, Yes, my soul and my [f]body! For my life is spent with grief, And my years with sighing; My strength fails because of my iniquity, And my bones waste away."

I know people who memorialize and grieve decades past the loss of a loved one. I'm not saying you can't miss that person. But God never intended for it to consume us.

I agree that grief is a process and takes time. I also think tragic and traumatic circumstances around death can affect the healing process. It will look different for different people. My encouragement to you is – why NOT break unhealthy soul ties with the one you've lost? Why NOT ask God to bless the healthy soul ties you had with them?

Think about this scripture: Proverbs 16:24, *"Pleasant words are like a honeycomb, Sweetness to the soul and health to the bones."*

This is a great example of how the soul is affected by POSTIVE things like positive words. And this scripture clearly states that that sweetness to the soul provides health to the bones.

Death can be more than the death of a person, like death of a marriage or a friendship. It can also allude to the extreme weight we carry when we are working in extreme emotional situations. I have prayed this prayer with so many different professionals. Lawyers, doctors, nurses, EMTS, counselors, CPAs, pastors, educators, politicians, hair stylists, even construction project managers.

No matter the circumstance, God will deliver you from the ties that bind you.

Psalm 119:28 *"My soul melts from heaviness; Strengthen me according to Your word."* (NKJV)

Chapter 4
Soul Maintenance

The key to a healthy soul is maintenance. You wouldn't rebuild a car engine and ignore simple maintenance, right? That would mean more work later and the car would lose its ability to run well deeming it untrustworthy on the road. You wouldn't build a house and fail to do simple maintenance so it could function as intended and maintain its value, right?

Maintenance? Sounds like a strange word to use when addressing a spiritual situation that is so strongly rooted in the mind and emotions but think about it. Our spirit is the engine that drives us, but the soul is the transmission. The soul (our mind, will, and emotion) will determine how slow, fast, or smooth we go – and every transmission requires maintenance.

As I've shared, highway time seems to work for me. However, where you do soul maintenance doesn't matter. What matters is that you actually conduct soul maintenance regularly. Go down the list. Pray over your spouse, your kids, your work colleagues. Pray over your extended family and friends. Pray over your church relationships.

I jokingly share when I am teaching about soul ties that we have soul ties with anyone with whom we share oxygen!

I do this because I want to be the best wife, mom, sister, friend, and leader that I can be. I don't have time anymore to waste on unhealthy issues. So, maintenance keeps my spiritual engine revved and ready for whatever the Lord has for me to accomplish.

I never want to be hindered in His plans for me again because I am drowning in soul issues!

It's been 10 years since I asked started asking Him to help me with soul ties and I've never looked back.

I hope this little book helps you improve the quality of your day-to-day living. If you feel that you need to go deeper into the soul than soul ties, I encourage you to read my book *The Wounded Warrior*. In that book, I teach about soul wounds (much deeper soul issues) and how to heal from them.

I would love to hear your stories. You may reach out to me at charli@active-faith.com.

Warning – Be Aware of Counterfeits

There are branches of mysticism, new ageism, and other religions that have taken the concept of soul ties and turned this concept into part of their meditation and healing practices. There are chakra cleansing exercises, cord cutting ceremonies, and hand binding rituals just to name a few. There are also vows and incantations used in witchcraft to evoke soul ties.

You will notice that the only thing really needed in breaking soul ties, biblically, is GOD. Since he created the soul (Gen. 2:7) with his own breath, he will redeem the soul as we see in Psalm 49:15 *"But God will redeem my soul from the power of the grave, For He shall receive me."* His grace is sufficient!

Counterfeits will require ceremony, ritualism, and mystical elements. Remember, the enemy wants to exploit and distort all things of God in order steer us onto the wrong path. Use discernment and be blessed!

Other books by Charli Caraway

The Wounded Warrior is a journey through personal healing. Discover the wounded soul and the one thing needed to heal the soul!

Journals by Charli Caraway

You may contact Dr. Charli at
charli@active-faith.com

Made in the USA
Columbia, SC
24 February 2025